Manage Your Emotions

by Martha E. H. Rustad

PEBBLE
a capstone imprint

Pebble Explore is published by Pebble, an imprint of Capstone
1710 Roe Crest Drive
North Mankato, Minnesota 56003
www.capstonepub.com

Library of Congress Cataloging-in-Publication Data
Names: Rustad, Martha E. H. (Martha Elizabeth Hillman), 1975- author.
Title: Manage your emotions / Martha E. H. Rustad.
Description: North Mankato : Capstone Press, 2021. | Series: Health and
my body | Includes bibliographical references and index. | Audience:
Ages 6-8 | Audience: Grades 2-3 | Summary: "Sometimes you feel
happy. Sometimes you feel sad. Sometimes you don't know how you
feel. You feel lots of different things all day long. Talk about your feelings
and learn how to deal with them"— Provided by publisher.
Identifiers: LCCN 2020027222 (print) | LCCN 2020027223 (ebook) |
ISBN 9781977132192 (hardcover) | ISBN 9781977133229 (paperback) |
ISBN 9781977154613 (pdf)
Subjects: LCSH: Emotions—Juvenile literature.
Classification: LCC BF723.E6 R87 2021 (print) | LCC BF723.E6 (ebook) |
DDC 155.4/124—dc23
LC record available at https://lccn.loc.gov/2020027222
LC ebook record available at https://lccn.loc.gov/2020027223

Image Credits
Shutterstock: Africa Studio, 27, antoniodiaz, 17, Art_Photo, 23, Boris
Medvedev, 6, Evgeny Atamanenko, 5, Kite_rin, 11, Kleber Cordeiro,
21, Lopolo, 8, Michael C. Gray, 15, Monkey Business Images, 4, 7, New
Africa, 9, Refat, 25, photonova, design element throughout, pixfly,
Cover, 24, Pressmaster, 13, Rawpixel.com, 29, Roman Bodnarchuk, 12,
seamind224, 26, Torychemistry, 18

Editorial Credits
Editor: Christianne Jones; Designer: Sarah Bennett; Media Researcher:
Morgan Walters; Production Specialist: Laura Manthe

All internet sites appearing in back matter were available and accurate
when this book was sent to press.

Printed in the United States   5002

Table of Contents

Emotions and Feelings......................... 4

Happiness..................................... 8

Sadness 12

Anger... 16

Scared and Worried 20

Calm 24

Glossary 30

Read More............................. 31

Internet Sites 31

Index 32

Bold words are in the glossary.

Emotions and Feelings

Everyone has feelings. You feel lots of different things all day long. You feel sad when a friend can't play with you. You feel happy when you play a game with your family. All **emotions** are OK.

Sometimes people act on their feelings. A mad person might hit something. A sad person might cry. A happy person might laugh. Your own actions can make a big difference on how you feel.

People often share their emotions with others. Talking about your feelings can make you feel better. It might also help you learn how to deal with them.

Some emotions last a long time. You love your pet for years. You love your family forever.

Sometimes emotions go away quickly or come and go. You feel **nervous** while you wait for your event. But once your turn comes, your nerves go away.

Some feelings are big. You feel sad about summer ending. Other emotions are small. You feel proud that you solved a tough math problem.

We can learn how to handle emotions. Think about a time you felt a strong emotion. How did your body feel? What was on your mind? How did you act?

Happiness

When you are happy, you feel joyful. People like to share this emotion. They feel cheerful on the inside. They want everyone to know. You feel proud that you learned to ride your bike. You feel excited that it is your birthday!

There are many ways to share joy. You can smile. A smile tells others that you feel happy. You can laugh. When people hear laughter, they want to laugh too.

People sometimes act out too much when they feel joy. You might talk too loudly. You might act too silly. It can be hard to settle yourself down if you get too wild.

If you start to feel wild, take a deep breath. Stop moving for a moment. Let yourself feel happy. But try to stay in control of your body.

Share your joy in a healthy way. Draw a colorful picture. Sing a happy song. Give a friend a hug.

Sadness

When you are sad, you feel unhappy. Everyone feels sadness. You might feel sad if you get hurt. If you fall down and skin your knee, you might cry.

You can also feel sad when your feelings get hurt. Your sister might call you a mean name. Your friends might leave you out.

People show sadness in many ways. Some people cry. Their cheeks might turn red. Some people get very quiet.

It is OK to feel sad and cry sometimes. But some people cannot cheer up. They might feel sad for a long time. This is not healthy.

We can learn healthy ways to show sadness. Ask someone for a hug. Write down your feelings. Ask a trusted adult or a good friend for help.

Anger

When you are angry, you feel mad. You might get mad about losing a game. Someone can feel angry if they have to do a chore. You can feel upset if you cannot do what you want.

Angry people show that they are mad. Their face might get red. They might shout. Their body might get **tense**.

Everyone feels mad sometimes. It is normal. But we have to find healthy ways to show anger.

When you feel mad, it is not OK to hurt people. Find a way to calm down. You can try lots of different things.

Sit still with your legs crossed. Close your eyes and try to **relax**. Put your hands on your stomach. Take a deep breath. Count slowly to 10. If you still feel mad, try punching a pillow. That gets your anger out.

See if you can find a **solution** to the problem. If not, it is OK to walk away. Come back and try again when you feel calmer.

Scared and Worried

When you are scared, you feel fear. People can be scared of real things. You might be afraid to get a shot at the doctor. You can feel worried before taking a test.

People sometimes feel afraid of things that are not real. Someone might worry that there is a monster under their bed. Some people get scared of a book or movie.

You show that you are scared or worried in many ways. Sometimes your body shakes. Your teeth might chatter. You might cry. You might not be able to sleep.

It is normal to feel scared or worried. But you must learn to deal with your fears. There are some ways to help yourself feel brave.

Think about what scares you. Then try to find a solution. You can always ask a teacher or a parent for help. Being **prepared** can help you fight your worries. If you are nervous for a test, study as much as you can.

Sometimes it helps to think of a funny way to solve a problem. If you are afraid of a monster, think about it tripping and falling down.

Calm

When you are calm, you feel peaceful. Your heart beats slowly and steadily. You breathe quietly.

People feel calm when they are safe. They may smile. It might feel good to talk. It might also feel good to stay quiet.

Some people like to be with friends or family when they feel calm. Other people like to be alone. They might go outside or take a walk.

When you feel calm, you know that things will work out. You can find ways to solve problems.

Some people do **yoga** to feel calm. This is a way of stretching and breathing that helps you relax. Other people feel calm when they read a book.

Listening to music can make you feel peaceful. You can listen to any kind of music that makes you feel happy. Sometimes dancing can make you feel calm too!

Everyone feels lots of emotions. A wide range of emotions is healthy. Think of your emotions like a rubber band. It can stretch way out. But it will break if it goes too far.

When you feel a strong emotion, take a moment to think about it. Breathe deeply. Count to 10. Find a healthy way to show how you feel.

Think about how your actions make other people feel. It is OK to show your feelings. But remember to be kind to others. You are in charge of your emotions.

Glossary

emotion (i-MOH-shuhn)—a way that you feel

nervous (NUR-vuhss)—to feel scared or worried

prepare (preh-PEHR)—to make yourself ready for something that you will be doing, or something that you expect to happen

relax (reh-LAKS)—to calm down

solution (suh-LOO-shuhn)—a way to solve a problem

tense (TENS)—tight

yoga (YOH-guh)—exercises and ways of breathing that keep the mind and body healthy

Read More

Christelis, Paul. *Exploring Emotions: Everyday Mindfulness.* Minneapolis: Free Spirit Publishing, 2018.

Cooper, Abby. *I Feel Anxious.* Minneapolis: Jump!, 2021.

Heneghan, Judith. *All Kinds of Feelings.* New York: Crabtree Publishing, 2020.

Internet Sites

Managing Your Feelings
www.cyh.com/HealthTopics/HealthTopicDetailsKids.aspx?p=335&np=287&id=1580

Peace Out: Guided Relaxation for Kids
www.safeYouTube.net/w/zeN1

Talking About Your Feelings
www.kidshealth.org/en/kids/talk-feelings.html

Index

afraid, 20, 22
angry, 16

brave, 22
breathing, 10, 19, 24, 26, 28

calm, 19, 24, 25, 26, 27
count, 19, 28
cry, 5, 12, 13, 14, 21

dance, 27
draw, 10

excited, 8

fear, 20, 22

happy, 4, 5, 8, 9, 10, 27
hug, 10, 14

joy, 8, 9, 10

laugh, 5, 9
love, 6

mad, 5, 16, 19
music, 27

nervous, 6, 22

peaceful, 24, 27
proud, 7, 8

quiet, 13, 24

read, 26
relax, 19, 26

sad, 4, 5, 7, 12, 13, 14
safe, 24
scared, 20, 21, 22
shout, 16
sing, 10
sleep, 21
smile, 9, 24
stretch, 26, 28

talk, 5, 10, 14, 24

unhappy, 12
upset, 16

walk, 19, 25
worried, 20, 21, 22
write, 14

yoga, 26